This book
is a hug

This book

is a hug

Comforting Wisdom for Difficult Days

Molly Reade

WORKMAN PUBLISHING · NEW YORK

Workman
Workman Publishing
Hachette Book Group, Inc.
1290 Avenue of the Americas
New York, NY 10104
workman.com

Workman is an imprint of Workman Publishing, a division of Hachette Book Group, Inc. The Workman name and logo are registered trademarks of Hachette Book Group, Inc.

Design by Remy Chwae

The publisher is not responsible for websites (or their content) that are not owned by the publisher.

The Hachette Speakers Bureau provides a wide range of authors for speaking events. To find out more, go to hachettespeakersbureau.com or email HachetteSpeakers@hbgusa.com.

Workman books may be purchased in bulk for business, educational, or promotional use. For information, please contact your local bookseller or the Hachette Book Group Special Markets Department at special.markets@hbgusa.com.

Library of Congress Cataloging-in-Publication Data is available.

ISBN 978-1-5235-3174-5 (paperback)
ISBN 978-1-5235-3175-2 (ePub)

First edition August 2025

Printed in Dongguan, China (06/25) APS.

10 9 8 7 6 5 4 3 2 1

This book
is a hug

This book is a hug

It's a soft blanket on a chilly night
It's a hot bath with lavender salts
It's the call of a single bird before dawn
It's a comfy sweatshirt that's been
    washed a hundred times

This book is a babbling brook by
    the window
It's a cozy robe just out of the dryer
It's the night sky with one bright star
It's your favorite song on repeat
It's a bowl of chicken noodle soup
It's a crackling fire

This book is a hug ♥

You've got a friend in me.

—RANDY NEWMAN

Nothing can dim the light which shines from within.

—MAYA ANGELOU

The way I see it,
if you want
the rainbow,
you gotta put up
with the rain.

—DOLLY PARTON

Always forgive
your enemies.
Nothing annoys
them so much.

—OSCAR WILDE

When you don't know what
to do, do nothing. Get quiet so
you can hear the still, small voice—
your inner GPS guiding you
to true north.

—OPRAH WINFREY

You make
the world
special just
by being
in it.

I'll be there for you
When the rain starts to pour
I'll be there for you
Like I've been there before
I'll be there for you
'Cause you're there for me too.

—THE REMBRANDTS

You are the sky.
Everything else is
just the weather.

—PEMA CHÖDRÖN

When you take time to
replenish your spirit,
it allows you to serve others
from the overflow.
You cannot serve from
an empty vessel.

—ELEANOR BROWN

You yourself,
as much as
anybody in the
entire universe,
deserve your love
and affection.

—SHARON SALZBERG

Difficult roads
often lead to
beautiful
destinations.

Don't judge each day by the harvest you reap but by the seeds that you plant.

—ROBERT LOUIS STEVENSON

The flower
that blooms in
adversity is the
most rare and
beautiful of all.

—FROM DISNEY'S *MULAN*

When it is
dark enough,
you can see
the stars.

—RALPH WALDO EMERSON

Almost everything will work again if you unplug it for a few minutes— including you.

—ANNE LAMOTT

Every strike
brings me
closer to
the next
home run.

—BABE RUTH

Sometimes
I think the only
thing worth
saying is
"I love you."

—SYLVIA BOORSTEIN

Sometimes we choose our battles. Sometimes our battles choose us.

Angels come in many shapes and sizes, and most of them are not invisible.

—MARTHA BECK

We're here for a reason. I believe a bit of the reason is to throw little torches out to lead people through the dark.

—WHOOPI GOLDBERG

Say what you wanna say
And let the words fall out
Honestly,
I wanna see you be brave.

—SARA BAREILLES

You are braver than
you believe, stronger
than you seem,
and smarter than
you think.

—CHRISTOPHER ROBIN TO POOH,
A. A. MILNE

An early morning walk is a blessing for the whole day.

—HENRY DAVID THOREAU

Keep your face always toward the sunshine, and shadows will fall behind you.

—WALT WHITMAN

Take all the time
you need.

It's okay to have
a meltdown.
Just don't unpack
and live there.

—HODA KOTB

The earth provides
us a brand new
beginning every
twenty-four hours.
It is a repeated
invitation to breathe
in the cool morning
air and start afresh.

—RICHELLE E. GOODRICH

Offer a gift to
the world no
one else can
offer: yourself.

—GLENNON DOYLE

Nothing is more beautiful than the smile that has struggled through the tears.

—DEMI LOVATO

No matter how hard the past, you can always begin again.

—JACK KORNFIELD

On the other side of a storm is the strength that comes from having navigated through it.

—GREGORY S. WILLIAMS

Be kind to
yourself.
You deserve
gentleness.

Lean on me
When you're not strong
And I'll be your friend
I'll help you carry on.

—BILL WITHERS

It's not about
getting over
things, it's about
making room
for them.

—BRIANNA WIEST

One small crack
does not mean that
you are broken.
It means that you
were put to
the test and you
didn't fall apart.

—LINDA POINDEXTER

Even darkness
must pass.
A new day will
come. And when
the sun shines,
it will shine out
the clearer.

—J.R.R. TOLKIEN

Even when we're apart,
I'll always be with you.

—POOH TO PIGLET, A. A. MILNE

Good friends
help you find
important things
when you've lost
them: your smile,
your hope, and
your courage.

—DOE ZANTAMATA

People who wonder if the glass is half empty or half full miss the point. The glass is refillable.

*I carry your
heart with me
(I carry it in my heart)*

—E. E. CUMMINGS

I would love to live
Like a river flows,
Carried by the surprise
Of its own unfolding.

—JOHN O'DONOHUE

It does not matter how slowly you go as long as you keep moving.

—CONFUCIUS

Live with the anticipation that something incredible might happen at any time.

—SHARON GANNON

New beginnings are often disguised as painful endings.

—LAO TZU

Yesterday is history,
tomorrow is a mystery,
today is a gift—that's why
we call it the present.

—AMERICAN PROVERB

Feel your
feelings.
Call anytime.
I'm here for
all of it.

What doesn't kill you
Makes you stronger.

—KELLY CLARKSON

Life isn't about waiting for the storm to pass. It's about learning to dance in the rain.

—VIVIAN GREENE

Look
inward—
the loving
begins
with you.

—OPRAH WINFREY

I believe, because I've done a little of this myself, pretending to be courageous is just as good as the real thing.

—DAVID LETTERMAN

Be proud
of how
hard you
are trying.

*Vulnerability
is the birthplace of
innovation, creativity,
and change.*

—BRENÉ BROWN

You cannot swim
for new horizons
until you have the
courage to lose
sight of the shore.

—WILLIAM FAULKNER

We don't even know how strong we are until we are forced to bring that hidden strength forward.

—ISABEL ALLENDE

Sometimes the people around you won't understand your journey. They don't need to, it's not for them.

—JOUBERT BOTHA

Just for now.
Find a corner
of your soul
that feels good.
Rest there.

—JAIYA JOHN

You are not a
drop in
the ocean.
You are the
entire ocean
in a drop.

—RUMI

In difficult
times we
learn, finally,
to take care
of ourselves.

There is always light.
If only we're brave enough to see it.
If only we're brave enough to be it.

—AMANDA GORMAN

Faith is belief
in what you
cannot see or
prove or touch.
Faith is walking
face-first and
full-speed into
the dark.

—ELIZABETH GILBERT

It's never overreacting to ask for what you want and need.

—AMY POEHLER

To love
oneself is the
beginning
of a lifelong
romance.

—OSCAR WILDE

Life is about balance. The good and the bad. The highs and the lows. The piña and the colada.

—ELLEN DEGENERES

Sometimes
your joy is
the source of
your smile, but
sometimes your
smile can be
the source of
your joy.

—THICH NHAT HANH

It's okay
not to
be okay.

Make your own kind of music
Even if nobody else sings along.

—BARRY MANN & CYNTHIA WEIL

The moments that make life worth living are when things are at their worst and you find a way to laugh.

—AMY SCHUMER

Life is like an ever-shifting kaleidoscope—a slight change, and all patterns alter.

—SHARON SALZBERG

Winter, spring, summer or fall,
All you have to do is call,
And I'll be there, yes I will
You've got a friend.

—CAROLE KING

Slow down. Don't allow others to hurry your healing.

—BEAU TAPLIN

You cannot prevent the birds of sorrow from flying over your head, but you can prevent them from building nests in your hair.

—CHINESE PROVERB

It's easier to ride the waves of emotion—even the rough ones— than to fight your way out of them.

My dark days
made me strong.
Or maybe I
already was
strong, and they
made me prove it.

—EMERY LORD

When things are shaky and nothing is working, we might realize that we are on the verge of something.

—PEMA CHÖDRÖN

The wound
is the place
where
the light
enters you.

—RUMI

*For good times and bad times
I'll be on your side forever more
That's what friends are for.*

—CAROLE BAYER SAGER &
  BURT BACHARACH

The best way out is always through.

—ROBERT FROST

Storms make trees take deeper roots.

—DOLLY PARTON

This too shall pass.

When you are in doubt,
be still, and wait.

—PONCA CHIEF WHITE EAGLE

We delight in
the beauty of the
butterfly but rarely
admit the changes
it has gone through
to achieve that
beauty.

—MAYA ANGELOU

Go back and take care of yourself. Your body needs you, your perceptions need you, your feeling needs you. The wounded child in you needs you. Your suffering needs you to acknowledge it.

—THICH NHAT HANH

When someone asks me why I cry so often, I say, "For the same reason I laugh so often—because I'm paying attention."

—GLENNON DOYLE

For me, singing sad songs often has a way of healing a situation. It gets the hurt out in the open, into the light, out of the darkness.

—REBA MCENTIRE

When you come out of the storm you won't be the same person who walked in.

—HARUKI MURAKAMI

Life is tough, but so are you.

Shower the people you love with love
Show them the way that you feel
Things are gonna be much better
If you only will.

—JAMES TAYLOR

I never regret anything. Because every little detail of your life is what made you into who you are in the end.

—DREW BARRYMORE

To the mind
that is still,
the whole
universe
surrenders.

—LAO TZU

*You are the stillness
beneath the mental noise.
You are the love and joy
beneath the pain.*

—ECKHART TOLLE

*Don't go back over your life
with a red pen.*

—GARY GULMAN

Do not apologize
for crying.
Without this
emotion, we are
only robots.

—ELIZABETH GILBERT

Admitting when you're not feeling strong is a special kind of strength.

Crying is like a thundershower for the soul. The air feels so wonderful after the rain.

—BRYANT MCGILL

The greatest glory in living lies not in never falling, but in rising every time we fall.

—NELSON MANDELA

Never worry alone.

—DAN HARRIS

The only constant
in life is change.

—HERACLITUS

She stood in
the storm,
and when the
wind did not
blow her way,
she adjusted
her sails.

—ELIZABETH EDWARDS

The only meaningful thing we can offer one another is love. Not advice, not questions about our choices, not suggestions for the future, just love.

—GLENNON DOYLE

Offer yourself the same kindness and warmth you would offer anyone else.

There are years that ask questions and years that answer.

—ZORA NEALE HURSTON

Like tiny seeds with potent power to push through tough ground and become mighty trees, we hold innate reserves of unimaginable strength.

—CATHERINE DEVRYE

You never know
how strong you
are until being
strong is your
only choice.

—BOB MARLEY

Be patient toward all that is unsolved in your heart, and try to love the questions themselves.

—RAINER MARIA RILKE

Shake it off,
Shake it off

—TAYLOR SWIFT

Magic exists if
you allow it. If
you open yourself
up to it.

—SANDRA BULLOCK

When nothing is going is going right . . . go left.

Pause for a few moments throughout the day to marvel at what's not broken.

—KRISTIN NEFF

*It's incredible where you can
go in your imagination.*

—ELMO

Nothing cures like time and love.

—LAURA NYRO

I've been searching
for ways to heal
myself, and I've found
that kindness
is the best way.

—LADY GAGA

Just because
someone
carries it well
doesn't mean it
isn't heavy.

Everyone
should have
their mind
blown at least
once a day.

—NEIL DEGRASSE TYSON

I get by with a little help from my friends.

—JOHN LENNON &
 PAUL MCCARTNEY

Show a little faith,
there's magic in the night.

—BRUCE SPRINGSTEEN

Everything bad that's ever happened to me has taught me compassion.

—ELLEN DEGENERES

Deep
breathing
is our nervous
system's love
language.

—DR. LAUREN FOGEL MERSY

Only when we are
brave enough to
explore the darkness
will we discover the
infinite power of
our light.

—BRENÉ BROWN

You are
doing a
great job.

Behind every
strong person
is a story that
gave them
no choice.

—PAULO COELHO

Look at the sky; remind yourself of the cosmos. Seek vastness at every opportunity . . .

—MATT HAIG

When we open
to the reality of
what is, even if
we don't like what
is, it helps almost
immediately.

—KRISTIN NEFF

Oaks grow strong in contrary winds, and diamonds are made under pressure.

—PETER MARSHALL

Fall down seven times, stand up eight.

—JAPANESE PROVERB

When friendships
are real, they are
not glass threads or
frost work, but the
solidest things we
can know.

—RALPH WALDO EMERSON

No matter how
you feel right now,
you look like
sunshine to me.

If you can't fly then run, if you can't run then walk, if you can't walk then crawl, but whatever you do you have to keep moving forward.

—DR. MARTIN LUTHER KING JR.

Slow breathing is like
an anchor in the midst of
an emotional storm:
The anchor won't make
the storm go away, but it
will hold you steady
until it passes.

—RUSS HARRIS

Breathing in, I calm
body and mind.
Breathing out, I smile.

—THICH NHAT HANH

Grief and resilience live together.

—MICHELLE OBAMA

In time,
yesterday's
red light
leads us to
a green light.

—MATTHEW MCCONAUGHEY

If you live long enough, you realize that so much of what happens in life is out of your control, but how you respond to it is in your control.

—HILLARY CLINTON

Sigh it out,
scream it out,
sing it out.

There are no wrong turns, only unexpected paths.

—MARK NEPO

We do not have to become heroes overnight. Just a step at a time.

—ELEANOR ROOSEVELT

Here I stand
in the light of day
Let the storm rage on
The cold never bothered
me anyway.

—FROM DISNEY'S *FROZEN*

We are all old houses, altered by time and circumstances. Our lives are shaped by the good and the bad, and we take it all in and make it a part of us.

—ERIN NAPIER

Hope begins in the dark, the stubborn hope that if you just show up and try to do the right thing, the dawn will come.

—ANNE LAMOTT

Yesterday is gone
and its tale told.
Today new seeds
are growing.

—RUMI

Something
beautiful
is waiting
for you.

When you reach the end of your rope, tie a knot and hang on.

—AMERICAN PROVERB

Rest until you feel like playing,
then play until you feel like resting.

—MARTHA BECK

*It is always darkest
just before the dawn.*

—THOMAS FULLER

There's always a sunrise and always a sunset, and it's up to you to choose to be there for it.... Put yourself in the way of beauty.

—CHERYL STRAYED

The mind is like tofu. It tastes like whatever you marinate it in.

—SYLVIA BOORSTEIN

The most beautiful people we have known are those who have known defeat, known suffering, known struggle, known loss, and have found their way out of the depths.

—ELISABETH KÜBLER-ROSS

Even walking
slowly can create
a breeze.

Peace comes when our
hearts are open like the sky,
vast as the ocean.

—JACK KORNFIELD

There is a crack
in everything.
That's how the light gets in.

—LEONARD COHEN

Light is in
both the
broken bottle
and the
diamond.

—MARK NEPO

If you suddenly and

unexpectedly feel joy,

don't hesitate.

Give in to it.

—MARY OLIVER

When the winds
of change blow,
some people build
walls and others
build windmills.

—CHINESE PROVERB

The magic is inside you.
There ain't no crystal ball.

—DOLLY PARTON

Go where
you are loved.

What lies behind us and what lies ahead of us are tiny matters compared to what lies within us.

—HENRY DAVID THOREAU

I don't even know
who someone is until
I've seen how they
handle adversity.

—SHONDA RHIMES

Sometimes the most important thing in a whole day is the rest we take between two deep breaths.

—ETTY HILLESUM

Courage is not the absence of fear, but the capacity to act despite our fears.

—JOHN MCCAIN

I believe that tomorrow is another day, and I believe in miracles.

—AUDREY HEPBURN

There is a light that shines
beyond all things on earth,
beyond us all, beyond
heaven, beyond the
highest, the very highest
heavens. This is the light
that shines in our heart.

—CHANDOGYA UPANISHAD

The fact that something has happened to a million other people diminishes neither grief nor joy.

Your story is
what you have,
what you will
always have.
It is something
to own.

—MICHELLE OBAMA

Every day we are engaged
in a miracle which we don't
even recognize: a blue sky,
white clouds, green leaves,
the black, curious eyes of a
child—our own two eyes.

—THICH NHAT HANH

What the caterpillar calls the end, the rest of the world calls a butterfly.

—LAO TZU

Hard times don't create heroes. It is during the hard times when the "hero" within us is revealed.

—BOB RILEY

Be kind to your mind.

The soul always
knows what to do
to heal itself. The
challenge is to
silence the mind.

—CAROLINE MYSS

Staying positive does not mean that things will turn out okay. Rather it is knowing that you will be okay no matter how things turn out.

—GARTH ENNIS

Awakeness is found in our pleasure and our pain, our confusion and our wisdom, available in each moment of our weird, unfathomable, ordinary everyday lives.

—PEMA CHÖDRÖN

Try to put your happiness before anyone else's, because you may never have done so in your entire life.

—MARGARET CHO

Talk to yourself as you would to someone you love.

—BRENÉ BROWN

I was amazed that what I needed to survive could be carried on my back. And, most surprising of all, that I could carry it.

—CHERYL STRAYED

Just this moment,
just this hour,
just this day.

Everyone
shines, given
the right
lighting.

—SUSAN CAIN

If your compassion does not include yourself, it is incomplete.

—JACK KORNFIELD

If you fall . . . make sure you fall on your back. Because if you fall on your back, you can see up. And if you can *see* up, you can *get* up.

—HODA KOTB

Not until we are lost do we begin to understand ourselves.

—HENRY DAVID THOREAU

Not everything that is faced can be changed; but nothing can be changed until it is faced.

—JAMES BALDWIN

There is a
sacredness
in tears.
They are not
the mark of
weakness, but
of power.

—WASHINGTON IRVING

If you light
a lamp for
someone
else, it will
also brighten
your path.

"Toad," said Frog, "it's time to let go of our worries and embrace the beauty of friendship."

—ARNOLD LOBEL

A real friend is one who walks in when the rest of the world walks out.

—WALTER WINCHELL

Try to be
a rainbow
in someone
else's cloud.

—MAYA ANGELOU

Real change,
enduring change,
happens one step
at a time.

—RUTH BADER GINSBURG

A wonderful
gift may not
be wrapped
as you expect.

—JONATHAN LOCKWOOD HUIE

The secret of change is to focus all of your energy, not on fighting the old, but on building the new.

—SOCRATES

Strive to do less.
Give yourself a break.
Rest.

The world breaks
everyone and
afterward many
are strong at the
broken places.

—ERNEST HEMINGWAY

Turn your wounds into wisdom.

—OPRAH WINFREY

Sometimes our strengths lie beneath the surface . . . Far beneath, in some cases.

—FROM DISNEY'S *MOANA*

The dark does not
destroy the light;
it defines it. It's our
fear of the dark that
casts our joy into
the shadows.

—BRENÉ BROWN

The best time to plant a tree was twenty years ago. The second best time is now.

—CHINESE PROVERB

That is one good thing
about this world ...
there are always sure
to be more springs.

—L. M. MONTGOMERY

Some days are for moving forward, and some days are just for getting through.

"Pooh?" he whispered.

"Yes, Piglet?"

"Nothing," said Piglet, taking Pooh's paw. "I just wanted to be sure of you."

—A. A. MILNE

Even a wounded
world holds us,
giving us moments of
wonder and joy.

—ROBIN WALL KIMMERER

You don't have
to see the whole
staircase, just
take the first step.

—DR. MARTIN LUTHER KING JR.

The new
dawn blooms
as we free it.

—AMANDA GORMAN

Acceptance
is not defeat.
Acceptance is
just awareness.

—STEPHEN COLBERT

My happiness grows in direct proportion to my acceptance, and in inverse proportion to my expectations.

—MICHAEL J. FOX

The river flows
The clouds drift
The sun rises
Things change

I am the
one thing in life
I can control.

—LIN-MANUEL MIRANDA

You can be miserable
before you eat a
cookie and you can
be miserable after
you eat a cookie,
but you can't be
miserable while you
are eating a cookie.

—INA GARTEN

Never put off till tomorrow what you can do the day after tomorrow.

—MARK TWAIN

I believe that if life gives you lemons, you should make lemonade, and try to find somebody whose life has given them vodka, and have a party.

—RON WHITE

New beginnings are available to all of us over fifty times a year; they are called Mondays.

—BYRON PULSIFER

It's not whether you get knocked down, it's whether you get up.

—VINCE LOMBARDI

You probably could use a glass of water.

Whoever said money can't buy happiness simply didn't know where to go shopping.

—GERTRUDE STEIN

My therapist told me
the way to achieve
true inner peace is to
finish what I start.
So far I've finished
two bags of M&M'S
and a chocolate cake.
I feel better already.

—DAVE BARRY

The only way we will survive is by being kind. The only way we can get by in this world is through the help we receive from others. No one can do it alone.

—AMY POEHLER

Everything is waiting for you.

—DAVID WHYTE

This book is a stroll on a breezy beach

It's a ride home when you're sleepy

It's a soft pastel sunset

It's a nourishing smoothie with a berry

    on top

It's the cushiest slippers

It's a knowing smile from a good friend

It's the things that are hard to capture

This book is a long, warm, heartfelt hug ♥

Molly Reade writes about wellness, happiness, relationships, and many other subjects. She's a great believer in the power of words to elevate, evolve, and heal. She lives in New York's Hudson Valley.